"The poems in Linwood Rumney's *Abandoned Earth* record a life measured in seasons and the lifespans of dogs. Through a childhood practicing pitches with overripe fruit and leveling water pistols at the sun, to the loves and losses of adulthood, Rumney catalogues the wildness that still has a will. In this book, beauty persists like a love story, a desire you can't seem to shake or unlearn. Here is everything we deserve or want to. Here in these abandoned orchards, the apple is an image that never stops speaking, whether it is cut as a lesson or, with that terrible inevitability that waits for all of us, summoned by the ground."

—Traci Brimhall, author of *Our Lady of the Ruins*, winner of the Barnard Women Poets Prize

"In *Abandoned Earth*, Linwood Rumney creates a world both menacing and comforting at once. While wide-eyed with wonder at life's sorrows, joys and mysteries, he maintains an understated tone that enables him to relate even the strangest events with a measured and convincing voice. This beautifully written collection contains what few books of poetry manage: high spirits, a keen eye and, above all, an embracing wisdom."

—John Skoyles, *Ploughshares* Poetry Editor and author of *Suddenly Its Evening: Selected Poems*

"This wonderful first collection reveals Rumney as a poet of great tonal and formal range. It wields a poetics hewn from dull jackknives, unpolished stones, and harsh northeastern winters—as luminous and dangerous as the ice that breaks branches with its weight. Yet it also traverses warmer climates, startling with wry odes and candid wit, transforming every object of the mundane into *a startling and unlikely jewel.*"

> —Danielle Cadena Deulen, author of *Our Emotions Get Carried Away from Us*, winner of the Barrow Street Prize.

"I love the clarity and precision of Linwood Rumney's poems and his restrained yet intense voice. Intense because it is restrained, pressurized by his deft use of stanzaic structures and forms. Robert Frost and William Carlos Williams seem to be among his influences, but his voice and vision are clearly his own. Rumney writes about the natural world and the human world, and he sees in both of them a terrible *excess* and a brutal *lack*. But, as in "A Mystery on the Greyhound Bus," he also recognizes that *simple beauty persists*, like the finch feeding her chicks in a bus station eave while a man on the platform, both laughing and crying, waves to a woman on the departing bus. Far more than simple beauty, that image—and Rumney's poetry throughout this book—is resonant and complex in the most compelling way."

> —Eric Nelson, judge and author of *Some Wonder: poems*

Abandoned Earth

Linwood D. Rumney

Winner of the Gival Press Poetry Award

Arlington, Virginia

Published by Gival Press, an imprint of Gival Press, LLC.

For information please write:
Gival Press, LLC
P. O. Box 3812
Arlington, VA 22203
www.givalpress.com

First edition
ISBN: 978-1-940724-09-6
eISBN: 978-1-940724-10-2
Library of Congress Control Number: 2016948933

Cover art: © Dimitris Kolyris | Dreamstime.com

Design by Ken Schellenberg.

Contents

for my father

The Ice Storm

It isn't tenderness that sometimes
compels water to press itself so firmly
against the landscape, like the too-cold hand
set upon a lover's belly to startle

and amuse. Trees break from the weight
of this embrace. As in spring, through
a trick of light, low-hanging branches
seem to fracture as they dip below

the river's surface. But there's no error
of appearance here. This season is literal.
Something lost all patience with shadows
and casts them out with clarity

that stuns for its accumulated
barrenness. Mornings, children skate
in driveways, parents gather ice to flush
toilets while the radio catalogs, as though

in war, the losses of the day before:
*one trailer collapsed, killing the sole
inhabitant. . .another bridge declared
impassable. . .and half the state cut off*

*from the power grid. Residents
are advised to boil water, to ventilate
running generators, to stay away
from windows and off the roads.* Later,

there will be interviews with the woman
who gave birth in a car flipped over
in a ditch, the octogenarian
who burned furniture for heat in his

living room, and the fortunate couple who,
visiting friends when the storm began,
were not at home when an ice swell
dragged the whole thing into the river.

Late Blossoms

Half the trees blossom in this old apple orchard.
The rest never bother, having died years ago
though they refused to lie down. Wolf River,
Empire, Red Delicious, even Crab Apple—

but no one comes to harvest this threadbare
abundance, except boys in late summer swinging
baseball bats at each other's wild pitches,
laughing at the acrid spray of unripened flesh.

And still later, after first frost, and after
the worst blizzard, haggard and starving deer
stagger in like old women at slot machines,
dredging for whatever meager fortune

they can claim. Come spring, it is easy to tell
the apples exploded by the boys' surplus
of violence from those gutted in the deer's
desperate hour. Where hoof and tooth could not

retrieve the fruit from winter, half-eaten apples
seem to bloom as the ice that held them recedes.
These small hemispheres emerge heavy and ruddy
with the bitter perfume of abandoned earth.

Burdocks

Along fence rows
      and road sides, first settlers
           of vacant parking lots,

displacing pavement the way
      early spring cracks ice,
           unmindful of our bodies'

sharp angles, they thrive
      despite bulldozers, wildfire,
           the gardener's murderous hands.

Even now their flowers
      seem foreign to New England.
           They're too round,

and the purple petals
      fading to brown
           seem strangely similar

to light—this perfectly
      inedible fruit is
           the sun's dull cousin.

You won't notice
      their mature bushes,
           up to your hip, the size

of a child, and as greedy.
        Only later, after recovering
                the terrain you know,

will you feel the sting
        of their need. And you tear,
                gouge this barbed fruit

from pant legs, shirt collar,
        shoe laces, even your hair.
                You see, they want

to be discovered this way.
        Despised, torn apart,
                sewn into your borders

by sudden anger,
        they're remade
                for your unmaking.

Approaching Night in the Country

i.

The sun impales itself
    with a sword while
        a blacksmith stretches

his freckled forearm across
    this forge to put away
        his bloody hammer.

ii.

Beyond the trees
    bodies shimmer
        at an empty altar.

Their heads tilt
    with an ear
        toward nothing.

iii.

A scarf draped over
     the horizon's neck,
         chimney smoke plumes

tangle, concealing
     winter's lecherous kiss,
         but the stench of pine

and cedar tells where
     they've been, what
         they've been doing.

iv.

The blacksmith retrieves
     his hammer—it glistens
         still, duller than before.

Rockland Harbor

From branches of the Wolf River Tree
my older brother calls my name, but not

any name the living know me by.
As a child I wandered this shore

searching for shells and strange stones.
I gathered fragments of cables tossed up

by the harbor and tapped a path
on the pavement to telegraph

my ellipsis home. As a child my brother
was too weak to climb trees. Swinging sticks

at brambles with their various shadows,
leveling water pistols at the sun

with its glistening thorns, he seemed uniquely
capable of enduring. It must be something

beside my brother making that racket,
an ugly bird's shadow laughing

at a bare branch. It must know how moon
calls the tide. If it's the claw the bird

carried from the sand, it must know
it was surrendered, permitting escape.

If it is, after all, an artifact
of my brother's voice, it must

sense how, with each fragrant breath,
these apples summon the ground.

First Dog

Chewing his leg
      as if a bitter
           stick keeps

fetching him,
      scratching his
           back on pavement

belly to air,
      and through grass,
           a willing servant

seeking—the fallen
      apple core probably
           tastes good to him.

The River

On the bank my dog recovers an eel.
His duty is to place it at my feet.

Head torn off, body lacerated
by the dam's turbines, its stench

is horrible. By instinct I fling it back.
My dog retrieves it. Years ago,

Danny and I discovered a nest
of eels in a boulder's eddy

upriver. We fished out all we could,
mutilated them with dull jackknives

and chucked the severed parts into
the river. We fished all morning,

frenzied by the spectacle of writhing
dismembered corpses, until he mistook

a vagrant head for a stone he meant
to launch at a decapitated body

still lurching through ripples.
The gaping jaw clamped hard

onto his ring finger, and Danny,
startled by this will to feed even

after death, gouged his own
knuckle to rip it off.

This headless and persistent
supplicant does not surprise me.

It seeks an audience to ask
after its reluctant groom.

The Benediction

Even as a boy I never liked to fish. But once
my uncle took me fishing on Silver Lake.

I caught two—the first an enormous pike,
half as long as I was tall. Cradling the beast

to test its strength, bewildered by the flash
of scale along its murky body, I twisted

the hook from its jaw. It gasped, striking its fin
against my shoulder with the force of a shotgun

recoil. Flopping from my arms, its pallet tore
my hand. My uncle slammed the fish on the ice,

forcing open the jaw to expose rows
of razor teeth that could have claimed my fingers.

Folding my hand between his hands to wrap
the wounds, he chuckled, *Now you won't forget.*

He should have warned me of a fish's will.
But he was always happy, always drunk.

The second time my line jerked taut, I imagined
an even bigger fish, teeth jutting from its jaws

like haggard tombstones. I struggled a half hour
to wear it out. When the pole went slack, I cursed

the way my father cursed, certain the fish
had cut the line. But I reeled in a yellow perch,

no longer than my hand. It had swallowed
the hook. Slicing it open to retrieve

the line and proud to think that feigned patience
could transform my fear, I tossed the carcass

across the ice, muttering, *Now you'll never know*—
a benediction that neither fish nor uncle heard.

After the Blueberry Harvest

Across the road three workers burn the field
to yield blueberries, larger and sweeter
than what grows wild. In two years, it will be time

to harvest again, and I, fifteen, will work
there, but today I clamber through
the pear tree's gritty branches

in the front yard, through smoky haze
and day's heat, through fruit ripening golden
around me, tapering from branches

toward the ground, while workers assemble
to cultivate flame. One collects
loose brush to burn as another digs

shallow trenches to temper the fire.
A third drags his foot over the soil
to signal where burning must end.

I won't be one who masters fire this way—
scorching everything to the crowns
where roots plunge their tortuous hands

into sunlight. Burning until they
remain only as amputee palms sprouting
new fingers in a field growing dormant

as a cold ember. I'll be one who curves
close to the earth to gather the plant's blue wealth,
who will temper my body through the misery

of work, who will return home too tired to climb.
I'll be one to stand under this pear tree with its
nascent fruit, summoning the memory of this blaze.

Jo in Wyoming

Summertime, 1946.
The prairie grass sunbaked yellow.
From the back seat of a Packard—
silver flash of the dashboard,
wooden panel more richly textured
than any of his landscapes—
Hopper paints his wife Josephine
painting a mountain in Wyoming.

Jo, the only woman who modeled
for him after they married. Jo,
a virgin and an artist when they wed—
the template if not the muse for all
the Hopper women, mostly shown
nude—sagging breasts and
jowls and narrow hips—
as he sketched studies.

In her diaries, she reports
she burnt her leg on the stove
while strutting for *The Girlie Show.*
In the painting muscles tense
and glisten from the strain of heels
as the angry stripper twirls
a silk shawl—her nipples absurdly
redder than her hair. With Jo posing,

Hopper drafted countless women
crawling in and out of bed.
At the window, the flush cheeks
of Hopper's fantasies mock
our blushes. *It was entirely
for him*, she writes of sex,
and left her feeling *subnormal*,
especially *attacks from the rear.*

His lighthouses are all self-portraits,
she claims. *At Cape Elizabeth,
it was pitiful to see all the poor
dead birds that had run into them
on a dark night.* But in Wyoming,
with no harsh angle of sun,
Hopper reveals Jo in all her clothes
and all her pleasure. Hair tied up,

no sudden wind can hide her smile
as she glances at a mountain
too cluttered for Hopper's tastes.
Her husband's jacket tossed
over the seat to remind us who
the driver is, Jo appears neither
lonely nor alone as her brushstrokes
near a summit we cannot see.

Lessons on Captivity

My neighbor's
>   dappled-gray horse
>   >   always tested the fence

at the edge
>   of the field.
>   >   Better I remember

the swimming hole
>   down the road—
>   >   trying to catch

the smaller fish
>   with my hands—
>   >   the thrill and the terror

as one slipped,
>   smooth
>   >   through my fist.

Some Lullabies

On the second floor our neighbor
is beating his girlfriend again
while their child screams.
She begs him to leave the boy
alone. I know you have probably
heard this story before,
so I won't trouble you with details
of late night calls to police
and his promises
to break clean.
                        I am ten. Tonight
I have wet the bed again, risen
and showered, pulled the sheets
from the stained mattress
and flopped onto the couch
in my mother's bathrobe.
                        Strange
though it may seem, the rhythm
of this beating—the syncopated
thumps, the blunt bass of his fists
on her body or the wall, the child's
strained alto grown hoarse—all of this
lulls me back to sleep. Like you,
I've heard it before, but I know
that in a few hours he will tire
of this violence.
                        I'll stir only

when my mother comes home
and presses her cold hand
to my forehead. It reeks
of raw herring she gutted
and canned all night at the factory.
I pretend not to notice that she trembles,
not from worry, but the routine
of exchanging her strength
for a paycheck.
                    As she turns
from me, sprawled on the couch
and pretending to sleep, she will say
nothing of the damp sheets beside
the hamper. In this way
we grant each other the privacy
of our distinct shame.

Junkyard Communion

Sundays my sister Karen and I'd split
bags of penny candy in the junkyard
after raiding each room of our trailer
for loose change and Pepsi cans.
Climbing through the interiors
of gutted clunkers, we declared
truces that wouldn't last the day.
Our lips puckered from flavors—
sour patch, lemonhead, warhead,
airhead, sour belt, jawbreaker—
that named the failings of our mother's men.
We suffered them then—teeth clenched
until burning gave way to no taste—
so we wouldn't suffer them later. We
were happy, sliding through shattered
windshields of Ford Pintos and station wagons,
kicking cracked molding. We peered
over the dashboards' broken panels,
through cattails and foxtail barley,
listened through insect buzz and birds
chirping from radiator grills,
to soundless engines
that would take anyone nowhere.

A Child's Tyranny

Sometimes at night
        my sister called to me
                from across the hall.

I unbraided myself
        from the sheets
                and stumbled

in my underwear
        toward her bed
                with the force

of a bird summoned
        south for its first
                winter. With nothing

to say to each other,
        Karen and I were twin
                question marks lying

in the dark where
        no words yet overwhelmed
                the path between us.

At dawn our parents
        rose from their
                separate beds

to pry us apart,
        insisting we were
                too old to lie together.

Now when I think
        of my sister, I rage
                silent and sleepless

at thoughts
        of her bruises—
                her boyfriend in prison

again. I rage
        with the mute
                tyranny of a child

emerging into
        a language
                it refuses to understand.

My Grandmother's Prosthetic Breast

My grandmother never wore
her prosthetic breast. For weeks
it lay on her dining room table,
displacing the vase of silk tulips
and plastic baby's breath.

I hardly dared look at the glazed
areola and stuck-on nipple
that seemed harder for being
so baldly displayed. Determined
to reject the vision before me,

instead I saw breasts everywhere—
footrests, doorknobs, and tv sets—
until even the table became plumper
and rounder. The whole world
reconstructed with concentric breasts,

and breast fractals, repeated indefinitely,
indifferent to scale. Then, between
my visits, the prosthetic breast moved
to the coat rack, to hang from a cup
in the special brassiere that could

have made her look even and whole.
I considered donning the pair,
breast and brassiere, as though
borrowing a jacket and umbrella.
My grandmother's foil, I would flaunt

my excess as freely as the lack
she revealed—my grandmother,
who said, *When I take off my shirt,*
I see the face of an old man
winking as if we shared a joke.

Leave Me, My Daughter

> *"Flies don't enter a closed mouth"*
> —*a saying, translated by Gloria Anzaldúa*

My wife Mary and I are making tortillas.
She taught herself and wants to teach me.
I work dough with the rolling pin,
searching for the right balance
of force and repetition.

The two Spanish words Mary heard
from her mother: *dejáme* and *mijita*.

Otherwise she never spoke to her
in Spanish. She asks me to translate
literally—all that I am capable of.

When I am too cautious, dough dries
swollen at the edges, cracking
like chapped lips.

Dejáme.
From *dejar*, to leave or abandon,
to go from, as in *¡Dejáme en paz!*
Leave me.

When I press too hard,
dough sticks to the rolling pin,
forming oblong shells that split
from the circumference
toward the center.

Dejáme.
What her mother said
when she was too angry
to speak English.

Mijita.
From *mi* and *hija. My little*
daughter.

I will have to press hundreds
of tortillas to master the rhythm
that yields the perfect
and resilient thinness.

Mary sprinkles my efforts
with water, and with only her hands
flattens and stretches the dough,
kneading together torn seams.

Mijita.
What she said to call her close—
to press her into her body.

We eat tortillas hot from the skillet.
The silence of our chewing
scatters the texture
of what her mother said.

Reading to My Stepson

at the kitchen table, his favorite
book about volcanoes. I ask
if he remembers where lava
comes from. Four years old,

he smiles and says *No,* hops out
of his chair to gather an apple,
butter knife and cutting board.
Because he refuses to believe

the diagram represents
the Earth, we turn to this ritual
whenever we read the page
that displays the world's layers.

But this time he wants to do my work,
deepens his voice and says,
Let's pretend the Earth is an apple.
In gestures he might recognize

as his, I stitch my brow, purse
my lips, insist the world
is not an apple. In his own voice
he responds, *It is! We're pretending*

we live here. I steady the apple
as the table shakes from his fury,
grab the knife as it rocks to the floor.
I study the apple, the glint of its skin

scarred only by the legacy of its birth—
the stem and the sepal's ashen star.
I consider how often we stand in
for each other's excess and absence—

stepson, stepfather, apple. He reaches
for the knife again, but this time I wield it
myself. I carve into the skin as the clear
froth of its juice brings him our song:

> *Cracks and holes*
> *All over the globe.*
> *That is how*
> *The lava gets out.*

He repeats without song,
I don't know where it comes from,
as I cut a wedge of the apple,
the Earth for him anyway.

Cloud Shadows

Winslow Homer, oil on canvas, 1890

On the deck of a wrecked ship cast up
by surf, a young woman and old fisherman
sit under cloud shadows at low tide

to forecast the reunion of beach grass
and sea. His back curves toward
the berm like the crest of a falling wave.

She sits upright on the bow, but seems
to tilt with the wind as behind her
the beach grass bends. It is impossible

to say if clouds gather toward a storm
or break above. His yellow beard
and fisherman's cap obscure his face.

Her eyes gleam as she smiles
for this man briefly forgotten
by the sea. It's as though she strolled

from the grass, he rose from the waves
to pass a moment together on sand laid bare
by this weather. Maybe a storm is coming,

and dark clouds will force their departure.
She'll recede through the grass as he hefts
his fishing net, casting to gather the wind

as rain scares fish into deeper water.
No one will notice as waves surge
and turn inland again, splashing

at the edge of the backshore between
beach grass and tide, where
they murmur stories into the sand.

Edible by Analogy

Do we harvest tomatoes to savor the garden?
If we pull out the words will the poem remain?
Like water in winter, light's surface hardens
when the bowl becomes the soup it contains.

If our words are lost, will their rumors remain?
Do tomatoes ripen near an empty breadbox
when our bowls become the spoons they contain?
We abandon unlit rooms that nothing unlocked

as tomatoes ripen near an empty breadbox.
Silverware eclipses the table eating the moon:
we abandoned unlit rooms—nothing unlocks.
We fled houses that fill up with our rooms.

Silverware eclipses the table, eating the harvest
like water in winter, even light hardens;
we flee houses filled with our rooms,
as we spoil the garden to savor the moon.

Daily Bread

No music allowed in the bakery
where I work—the baker's zealous speech
carries the morning cadence.
I, alone with him where
no natural light can enter, heft and deliver
bulk bags of flour, yeast, salt.

Over the hymn of industrial mixers that flash
like chain mail, he proclaims,
Of all things men make, bread is closest to God.

I shuffle between proofing stations
to oil and stack racks of bread pans,
building transient temples gleaming
a head taller than me—ready to receive
the daily dose of faith.

Have the workers of iniquity no knowledge?
he intones as the dough congeals,
folded and braided into itself
by the rhythm of the mixing blade—
*Who eat up my people as they eat bread,
and call not upon the Lord?*

We slap dawn's first dough
onto the cutting table as he repeats
that I am unfit to bake with him:
It takes belief first, then skill.
Lacking both, I grip the slicer,
crude in its perfectly rectangular shape,
and plunge it into the dull mass
before me, granting form to his faith.

Low Tide in Penobscot Bay

i.

At low tide, clam diggers
once peppered the mudflats,
punching gloved hands into
soggy clay. With almost
every jab they caught the deeper
briny stench and stony clams.

Now the mudflats are almost empty,
and divers dig in the bay for clams
that could once be summoned
by anyone with the will to make a fist.

ii.

A circus ferry once ran up and down
the coast, from Cape Cod to Bar Harbor—
with an elephant, a tiger, and an osprey
they claimed was an eagle—but the boat
caught fire leaving Searsport,
out past Deer Isle. The crew jumped ship first

then the circus performers,
then the animals. The elephant
couldn't take the cold,
and the osprey couldn't fly.
As the tide returned, fire consumed the ferry,
and water. Still, some people claim
the tiger made it to the island.

iii.

And now at low tide I walk
along the beach with my wife
as her son pokes through windrows
of seaweed, uncovering crabs
that lift their defiant claws

and skitter toward the water.
We come upon a jellyfish
cast up by surf, dead
but still poisonous—a dark
red, with tentacles folded under,
a ripe and formless gem.

Tributary

My hand lingers
        along your neck,
                a fallen limb

caressing headlong
        river water. This ruined
                timber remembers—

rain wears down mountains.

A Mystery on the Greyhound Bus

Sadness, like humor, is about timing.

The driver passes down the aisle,
collecting tickets. I follow the gaze
of the woman seated before me
to a man on the platform, laughing
and crying. And mouthing something
to her—I can't tell what.

He *cries* so hard
tears fog his bifocals.
He *laughs* so hard his
face glows crimson.

He laughs and points to the eave where a finch
feeds her chicks—such simple beauty persists.

He *laughs* so hard
tears stain his glasses.
He *cries* so hard his face
ignites like embers.

He's mouthing something I can't say—crying
and waving and pointing to the eave where
a finch feeds her chicks.
                    We must laugh
anyway, his trembling finger seems
to claim, *but how can the world go on*
in view of such imminent departure?

Bravo! Gentle and furious
man with your spectacles—
a double vision!

Bravo! Little bird
feeding your chicks
on time, whatever
the occasion.

Bravo! Woman whose expression
I can only guess at—your near
absence brought us together.

Second Dog

"The earth knows how to handle the great dead
Who lived the body out, and broke its laws"
—James Wright

This one's skull
        in a field
                isn't so great

after all.
        All summer
                she broke chains,

jumped fences,
        chased cattle until
                they kicked her,

until she bit
        our neighbor's
                Appaloosa, until

our neighbor
        started shooting we
                laughed we thought

he meant to miss.

After Seeing *Amour*

a broken prose villanelle

A few weeks after I watched my father die, I saw *Amour*. I almost wrote, "I made the mistake of seeing." I saw it because my fiancée, a Francophile who didn't know much about it either, chose it from the three options at the movie theater. Had I known a little more, I might have anticipated the cloying sentiment of something like *The Notebook*. A forbidden romance and a happy marriage. Peaceful simultaneous deaths for the loving couple. *Amour* has no flashbacks. We catch glimpses of the retired couple's long life together only through brief comments from the daughter and a photo album Anne (Emmanuelle Riva) scans.

It has been a few weeks since I watched my father die, so, right now, I feel like something of an expert on what death looks like. I know this kind of expertise is individual (it depends on the circumstances of the dying witnessed) and it partially fades, and it is expertise that all but the most stubborn among us must one day gain. In our last phone conversation, we discussed the weather. He was frustrated; he no longer had an appetite.

Anne's daughter says as a child she was comforted by the sound of her parents making love. Once Anne is wheelchair bound, her husband Georges must take over the domestic chores, possibly for the first time in his life. He is clumsy. He doesn't quite know where the salt is kept. When he washes the dishes, he fails to rinse them.

It has been a few weeks since I watched my father die. The day after we last spoke, he slipped into what the nurses called an "active dying phase," a phrase that struck me as a little silly, another bureaucratic oxymoron, but which I now see the logic of. I flew home. He never woke enough for another lengthy conversation, though he responded "yes" or "no" when my mother asked if he was in pain. If "yes," which almost always was the answer, she gave him two more drops of morphine. He started sweating heavily.

After Anne's first stroke, she couldn't pour a cup of tea. Another stroke makes her wet the bed. Except for some piano playing embedded in the script, *Amour* has no music. *Salière* is translated as *salt cellar*. It has been a few weeks since I watched my father die. He no longer answered the one question that still mattered: "Are you in pain?" We gave him morphine when we thought to ask. We changed his diaper. I passed the time staring at his neck, observing with pride as his heart raced and raced and raced. My mother told him *she* would be all right. *She* would feed his cat even though she hated it.

As I watched Anne die, I searched for signs of Riva. When surgery left Anne half paralyzed, I hoped to see Riva's fingers wiggle. After the last stroke took Anne's speech, I wanted Riva to betray, through a knowing glance, the syntax underneath the gibberish. My father slept, or seemed to, and snored heavily, as he always had. Then the snoring became a shallow gurgle. We gave him two more drops of morphine. We changed his diaper. We gave him a suppository for the fever.

It's been a few weeks since my father died. No one asks me anymore how I'm "holding up," for which I'm grateful. When someone tells me they are sorry for my loss, my grief flares like a spoiled child. I calmly take him by the hand and guide him to his bedroom. I close the door. I sip my coffee and pretend to read the newspaper as he screams to be let out. As I watched Anne die, I looked for Riva. I could not find her.

Skipping Stones on Penobscot River

Worried from bed
      I assemble my
            loose ends

to banish them all
      to this poem—
            unpolished stones

more common than
      stars together we
            toss on this river.

Morning Routine

He struts, indifferently nude, scratches
as pleases, gathers the skins of dead
chemical reactions for warmth only. How

he paws through the bush of the vegetable crisper
for berries as bright and round as the moon.
He gulps handfuls at a time without closing
his eyes. Now he forages

in the branches of the refrigerator
for the golden white eggs of birds
who plead each day with the sun
to stand guard over the unborn. Now he

cracks the eggs open. How he cooks them
slowly. Surely if there are beings observing
from the stars or the parking lot, they gaze
through his balcony window and think, longingly,

What a strange and curious creature. To glut
while fearlessly exposed in the yellow dirt
of his apartment, surrounded by tools
he did not make. To sop

the limpid yolks of sunny side eggs,
losing a little to his beard, letting it dribble
and harden to amber in the barren fields
of his golden breast.

Ode to Running Late

Worried that you left the stove on, you always endure burning visions
of the loss of all you know. You shout *Hold on!* and *Not yet!* as you
pat yourself down for glasses that are always already perched on
your head, as you dig absurdly for keys that are exactly where you
think.

The first time we bumped into each other, I didn't think we'd be such
good friends—just one or two idle conversations and then we'd
never meet again.

Now it seems I can't go anywhere without you—job interviews,
picking Mother up at the airport, whenever I go on a date.

You even drove me to my brother's funeral, though you never knew
him, insisting calmly, for once, they would understand—*it takes
time to get these moments right.*

Running Late, you have been wrong about many things—whom I
should marry, what careers I'm suited for...but about this one thing
you were right.

You're my most reliable excuse. No one wonders if I'm hungover, crying
for no good reason, or sleeping with someone I shouldn't if I claim to
have been visiting you.

Like a supervillain or prank caller, I cackle when I'm on my way,
glaring through eyes too large to hold anything but madness.

I call my nemesis, He Who Is Always On Time And Getting Things
Right The First Try, declaring in your husky, unmistakable tones

that *I*. . .

I am RUNNING LATE! And, as quick as epiphany I scurry between old women gathering kindling in the Whole Foods parking lot. I bound obliquely across Cambridge Street, dodging cars truly lost to the dull blare of their horns, fearlessly flipping off any who would delay me further. . .

Until, at the door of the Thirsty Scholar Pub, I tear off my sunglasses and wipe my brow, straighten my collar and press on.

I, Running Late, am certain that nothing will unfold as I have foreseen and that those who know me best will never believe I am who I say I am.

Third Dog

Ducks splash
      on the low
           water river.

The dog barks,
      wags, from her tail
           water spatters,

tracing
      an ampersand.
           Flopping

to the bank
      she scratches &
           twists a half

torus in mud.

Ode to Dreams

Oh how grateful I am when you come around with strange photographs
you claim I took, like the more sober friend the morning after a night
out who tells me how crazy and funny I was.

You don't visit often enough. You must love others better.

But how you make me laugh with your weird logic and crude jokes. A
cosmonaut frog? On the moon? Ha!

You disturb me, Dreams, with your reckless laws and wild lusts, your
perverse need to mingle anything with anyone. A crow with a man's
head? A drowning block of cheese I can never save?

When you press your wet tongue into my mornings, I can't tell my
nights from my days. What odd gifts you give! Only after you stop
sending them do I count them a blessing.

We told each other so many stories! Even now I try to repeat your
versions but always lose some detail I didn't know mattered—the
label on the shampoo bottle you held over the crater, the color of the
sky you rocketed through.

Dreams, you bore me. Why can't you just say what you mean? Why am
I always falling or flying or running away *from you?*

You know now and then I catch you eyeing me across a crowded bar.
Should I come up and say, *You look so familiar? You don't have to
be lonely tonight.* Or should I just let you admire me, however you
find me, happy that sometimes we meet in public, but mostly when
no one is looking?

Urban Self-Portrait

My hair is an ancient forest
north of the city—the oldest trees
have been cut down
and the native birds kicked out.

Warring pundits sit behind
my temples. They write
furiously all day
without citing additional research.

My neck traces a channel
draining a greater lake
into a lesser one.

Do so many lights
line my streets that my teeth gleam,
fiercely visible from orbit?

My genitals are revolutionaries
who take up arms only when
the capital is burning and the tyrant dead.

When will workers finish the new tunnel
so you may pass through me without
looking around?

The Boonie Hat

Creased on both sides, the full brim proves
even then my father, an army ranger
in Vietnam, squared the boundaries
of his vision through the hats he wore.

Standard issue in '69, made
of rip-stop cloth, leaf camo pattern,
it has black metal eyelets and mesh
ventilation screens, two on each side.

The label reads, *Hat, Camouflage,*
for Tropical Combat, Type II.
It's most frayed along the chinstrap where
his sweat and decades of attic storage

have worn the nylon-cotton cord.
This is the hat he loaned me for my travels
in Costa Rica because, he says,
The sun hits harder than you think.

Cooled by his vintage shade, I was
neither invading force nor listless tourist,
though I feared I might be both.
I wore it as I learned the layout

of San José, shielding my eyes
with auburn-tinted metal-rimmed
Aviator glasses. Absurdly dressed
in the military trappings of my father's

generation and thinking I'd camouflaged
my blue eyes, pale complexion
and straw-colored hair, I manufactured
my first ¡Buenos días! and ¿Dónde estoy?

I wore it again as I hiked three days
through the Cloud Forest to spend a week
at a tourist's lodge owned by an expat's son.
Seen by hawks from above, I wanted

to seem a forest pixel moving too slowly
to be of interest, and seen from the side
by howler monkeys screaming
between tree limbs, I wanted to be

the figure of a man distilled from leaf
to leaf. By day I earned my keep digging
a fish pond, and at dusk, we split
a bottle of whiskey as he recounted

stories of gelding stallions. His tongue
muffled by booze and trapped
between his father's homeland
and the only country he knew, he detailed

the knots used to keep the horse
from kicking, as the sun softened
behind clouds. Folded on my knee
my father's boonie hat hid nothing,

as my friend explained where to find
the seam, how to sever cords anchoring
organ to muscle, as the sun set,
splayed out and wincing beneath us.

Banana Workers in Limón, Costa Rica

Banana bunches suspended over their heads,
they run headlong for the packing house,
sprinting through the plantation's labyrinth

of cableway paths. They wear used
Yanquí clothes. Nike swooshes dangle
from their jerseys like broken wings.

They smirk at the two of us, a plump gringo
and a labor organizer, cradling clipboards
while we watch them toss the green pillars

onto the conveyor belt, chug a half liter
of water and dash again into these hectares
of plants so large they're mistaken for trees,

and so fragile they're held up against
the fierce weight of their own fruit, anchored
to the soil by the same twine binding

the workers' sneakers. I've read of a boy
who swallowed a pinch of fungicide-salted
earth on a dare, collapsing as though poisoned.

I've read of laid-off immigrants from Belize,
Panama, and Nicaragua who, ashamed
to return to families they can no longer feed,

end their lives with sips of paraquat—
their bodies, discovered weeks later,
untouched by scavengers or rot.

Sunlight scatters the long shadows of these
impostor trees. My companion yawns,
tugs at my elbow, says we should grab a beer,

some *gallo pinto*, no one wants to talk
today. From a mile out the road winds
around the valley's lip, an island of

pesticide-soaked bags shimmers and recedes
among green cascades of banana leaves—
a startling and unlikely jewel.

Translating Machado

Machado's best line, *hoy es siempre todavía*,
almost means, *today is forever yet always still.*

Lorca collapses as dawn cleaves Granada open.
A hammer pounds the sky. The earth, the anvil rings still.

Do you hear tombstones deflect the chestnut's hard rain?
Are they anxious? *As they germinate they fall still.*

After the raid on Trang Bang the "Napalm Girl" survived.
Screaming *Too hot!*, her flesh a tattered cloth, she fled still.

Everything behind her is burning, in the photo.
Even today Kim Phúc's eyes wax wide and hold still.

Do you recall Neda's last words? *I'm burning I burn.*
Iran's legato voice fills the street where she lies still.

No nomination could cancel your last appointment.
Tookie, aren't you too large to pass through death's door still?

Laviera says he could never translate *soledad*.
In English I divorce, in English I'm silent, still.

Listen, strangers often hear my surname is Linwood.
But no threshold can translate my end's dialect. Still.

Regarding My Youth

Regarding my youth, I am already
the ship captain's widow
who returns to the lighthouse less frequently.

Regarding my old age, I nervously
glance over my shoulder
like a stingy man at an ATM
in a poor neighborhood.

As for my loneliness,
I find traces of it
in the discarded
skin of a venomous snake.

As for my body, at night
I am awakened by the crash
of a vase. I scurry downstairs
to discover my son
has returned, resentful
and poor and contemplating death.

Regarding my death,
surgery reveals a sapling
rooted to my lung. I grow
wary of the other life nurtured
by my own breath.

After Passing a Picnic Table in a Cow Pasture

If I were a farmer,
    I too would display
        the present meal

before the future ones,
    mooing their curious
        indifference. I would

sit at a table
    that's made
        of the most

weathered wood.
    I would remind myself
        I deserve everything.

Acknowledgements

the Aurorean, "Skipping Stones in Penobscot River"

CircleShow, "The Ice Storm" and "Rockland Harbor"

Carolina Quarterly, "Low Tide in Penobscot Bay"

Coal Hill Review, "Leave Me, My Daughter"

Cold Mountain Review, "Some Lullabies"

Crab Orchard Review, "Banana Workers in Limón, Costa Rica"

Day One (Amazon Publishing), "Regarding My Youth"

Glass: A Journal of Poetry, "A Child's Tyranny"

The Hampden-Sydney Poetry Review, "The Benediction" and "Reading to My Stepson"

Harpur Palate, "Daily Bread" and "The Boonie Hat"

The Kenyon Review Online, "After Seeing Amour"

North American Review, "My Grandmother's Prosthetic Breast"

Ploughshares, "Junkyard Communion"

Poetry Quarterly, "Jo in Wyoming" and "The River"

The Potomac Review, "Translating Machado"

Puerto del Sol, "Second Dog"

Quercus Review, "Lessons on Captivity" and "Third Dog" (as "Note to a Future Paleontologist")

The Southern Review, "After Passing a Picnic Table in a Cow Pasture"

Superstition Review, "Late Blossoms"

Thieves Jargon, "Morning Routine"

Valparaiso Poetry Review, "After the Blueberry Harvest"

"Some Lullabies" also appeared in the anthology *What Poets See*, and "Low Tide in Penobscot Bay" also appeared in the anthology *Our Place* (FutureCycle).

"The Ice Storm," a finalist for the 39th New Millennium Literary Awards, also appeared in their 2016 anthology.

"Junkyard Communion" also appeared in *Intimacy: An Anthology* (Jacar).

"Third Dog" also appeared, as "Note to a Future Paleontologist," in the anthology *To Unsnare Time's Warp* (Main Street Rag).

I am grateful to Kimmel Harding Nelson Center, the St. Botolph Club, Anne Britting Oleson, Naomi Guttman, Daniel Tobin, and especially John Skoyles for mentoring me and nurturing this work. Critiques from Mary Kovaleski Byrnes, Sarah Sweeney, Rochelle Hurt, Les Kay, John Drury, and Sara Watson also shaped this book as a whole.

Thanks also to Anne Champion, Kent Leatham, Ron Spalletta, Kristen Hoggatt, Matt Summers, Joshua Hallsey, Matt Rich, Dathalinn

O'Dea, Daniel Heyman, Julia Koets, Brian Brodeur, Michael C. Peterson, Lisa Summe, and Akshay Ahuja for fellowship and feedback.

For the gifts of time, resources, and access to writing communities, I am grateful to the Writers' Room of Boston, the Wesleyan Writers Conference, the Stonecaost Writers Conference, the Colrain Manuscript Conference, Emerson College, the University of Cincinnati, and the Charles Phelps Taft Research Center.

Finally, thanks to Eric Nelson for selecting my work and to Eric, Danielle Cadena Deulen, John Skoyles, and Traci Brimhall for their generous assessments of it. Thanks to Robert L. Giron and the staff at Gival Press for their kindness and diligence. And, of course, for her boundless support and encouragement, I am indebted to my wife, Jessica Rae Hahn.

Notes

"Second Dog": The epigraph is from James Wright's "On the Skeleton of a Hound."

"Leave Me, My Daughter": The epigraph is from "How to Tame a Wild Tongue" in *Borderlands=La Frontera* by Gloria Anzaldúa.

"Daily Bread": "Have the workers of iniquity no knowledge? Who eat up my people as they eat bread and call not upon the Lord" is Psalms 53:4.

"Jo in Wyoming": The biographical information about Jo and Edward Hopper, including Jo's journal entries, were gleaned from *Edward Hopper: An Intimate Biography* by Gail Levin. According to Levin, the bulk of Josephine Hopper's art was destroyed by the Whitney Museum after her death.

"After Seeing *Amour*": The broken villanelle approach was inspired by Ron Spalletta's "Blank Villanelle."

"Ode to Running Late" is for Gregory Stenta.

"Translating Machado": The line from Machado is from "Proverbios y cantares" ("Proverbs and Songs") 38: "Mas el doctor no sabía / que hoy es siempre todavía" ("But the doctor didn't know / that today is forever still"). Kim Phúc was the subject of the famous "Napalm Girl" photo taken during a raid on Trang Bang in Vietnam by the Southern Vietnamese. Neda Agha Soltan was a singer who was shot on June 20, 2009 by an Iranian soldier while attending a protest in Tehran. The incident, including graphic footage of Neda's last moments, was caught on camera. Neda literally translates as "voice." Stanley

"Tookie" Williams, cofounder of the Crips, was sentenced to death in California for the murders of Albert Lewis Owens, Yen-Yi, Tsai-Shai, and Yu-Chin. While on death row, he renounced gang life and wrote memoirs and books for at risk youth warning them against gangs, for which he was nominated for the Nobel Prize in two categories, Peace and Literature, numerous times. The quote from Tato Laviera is from his poem "My Graduation Speech."

"Regarding My Youth": The last stanza alludes to the story of Artyom Sidorkin. While performing a biopsy for what was believed to be lung cancer, Russian surgeons found instead that Sidorkin had a 5 cm spruce sapling growing in his lung.

About the Author

Linwood Rumney's poems have appeared widely in journals, including *The Southern Review, Hotel Amerika, Puerto de Sol, New Millennium Writings, Ploughshares,* and *North American Review,* and they have appeared in the anthologies *Intimacy* (Jacar), *Weatherings* (FutureCycle), and *To Unsnare Time's Warp* (Main Street Rag), among others. Translations of Aloysius Bertrand, an early practitioner of the modern prose poem in French, have appeared in *Arts & Letters, Hayden's Ferry Review,* and elsewhere. An Associate Editor for Black Lawrence Press and a previous Poetry Editor for *Redivider,* he has received awards from the St. Botolph Club and the Writer's Room of Boston, as well as a residency from the Kimmel Harding Nelson Center. Originally from central Maine, he currently lives in Cincinnati, where he completed a PhD as a Charles Phelps Taft Fellow.

Poetry from Gival Press

Some Wonder by Eric Nelson
Songs for the Spirit by Robert L. Giron
Sweet to Burn by Beverly Burch
Tickets for a Closing Play by Janet I. Buck
Voyeur by Rich Murphy
We Deserve the Gods We Ask For by Seth Brady Tucker
Where a Poet Ought Not / Où c'qui faut pas by G. Tod Slone

For a complete list of Gival Press titles, visit: *www.givalpress.com*.

Books available from Follett, Ingram, Brodart, your favorite bookstore, on-line booksellers, or directly from Gival Press.

Gival Press, LLC
PO Box 3812
Arlington, VA 22203
givalpress@yahoo.com
703.351.0079